Contents

Warrior Elite

In the 8th century, the king of the Franks, Charlemagne, needed warriors that could travel and fight on horseback to conquer other lands and maintain his huge empire. In return for oaths of loyalty he gave them lands—and the medieval knight was born.

A Norman knight cuts down Anglo-Saxon King Harold II in 1066. The Norman conquest brought knights to England.

SERVICE

Knights were vassals, or servants, to noblemen called lords. The knights paid homage, or pledged loyalty, to their lords, promising to always honor them and do their will. The knight would rent his land to peasants, called villeins, and freemen. Some would repay the knight with military service, so he could call up a small army when needed.

Knights also had servants called squires—usually the teenaged sons of other nobles. Squires traveled with their knights and were trained

in how to become knights themselves. Ultimately, all peasants, squires, knights, and lords were vassals to the king, who owned most of the land. He called on them when wars had to be fought.

CHIVALRY

A knight had to be gallant and loyal, and swear against selfishness and cowardice—in other words, he had to be an excellent soldier. This code of chivalry included protecting the defenseless—widows, children, and elders (but not peasants).

Soldiers could be knighted for brave deeds or to give them courage before battle.

Graphic Medieval History

KNIGHTS

By Gary Jeffrey & Illustrated by Nick Spender

Crabtree Publishing Company
www.crabtreebooks.com

Crabtree Publishing Company
www.crabtreebooks.com
1-800-387-7650

Publishing in Canada
616 Welland Ave.
St. Catharines, ON
L2M 5V6

Published in the United States
PMB 59051, 350 Fifth Ave.
59th Floor,
New York, NY 10118

Printed in Canada/032014/MA20140124

Created and produced by:

David West Children's Books

Project development, design, and concept:

David West Children's Books

Author and designer: Gary Jeffrey

Illustrator: Nick Spender

Editor: Kathy Middleton

Production coordinator and

Prepress technician:

Ken Wright

Print coordinator:

Margaret Amy Salter

Photo credits:

p5 middle, Anagoria

Library and Archives Canada Cataloguing in Publication

Jeffrey, Gary, author
        Knights / Gary Jeffrey ; illustrator: Nick Spender.

(Graphic medieval history)
Includes index.
Issued in print and electronic formats.
ISBN 978-0-7787-0398-3 (bound).--ISBN 978-0-7787-0404-1
(pbk.).--ISBN 978-1-4271-7510-6 (html).--ISBN 978-1-4271-7516-8
(pdf)

        1. Knights and knighthood--Europe--History--Juvenile
literature. 2. Agincourt, Battle of, Agincourt, France, 1415--
Juvenile literature. 3. Orléans (France)--History--Siege, 1428-
1429--Juvenile literature. 4. Bosworth Field, Battle of, England,
1485--Juvenile literature. 5. Knights and knighthood--Europe--
History--Comic books, strips, etc. 6. Agincourt, Battle of,
Agincourt, France, 1415--Comic books, strips, etc. 7. Orléans
(France)--History--Siege, 1428-1429--Comic books, strips,
etc. 8. Bosworth Field, Battle of, England, 1485--Comic books,
strips, etc. 9. Graphic novels. I. Spender, Nik, illustrator II.
Title. III. Series: Jeffrey, Gary. Graphic medieval history.

CR157.J45 2014   j929.6   C2014-900361-7
                                        C2014-900362-5

Library of Congress Cataloging-in-Publication Data

Jeffrey, Gary.
 Knights / by Gary Jeffrey ; illustrated by Nick Spender.
    pages cm. -- (Graphic medieval history)
 Includes index.
 ISBN 978-0-7787-0398-3 (reinforced library binding : alk.
paper) -- ISBN 978-0-7787-0404-1 (pbk. : alk. paper) -- ISBN
978-1-4271-7510-6 (electronic html) -- ISBN 978-1-4271-7516-8
(electronic pdf)
1. Knights and knighthood--England--History--To 1500--
Juvenile literature. 2. Great Britain--History--Lancaster and
York, 1399-1485--Juvenile literature. 3. Knights and
knighthood--England--History--To 1500--Comic books, strips,
etc. 4. Great Britain--History--Lancaster and York, 1399-1485--
Comic books, strips, etc. 5. Graphic novels. I. Spender, Nik,
illustrator. II. Title.

 CR4529.G7J44 2014
 929.7'1--dc23

                                        2014002259

EQUIPPING A KNIGHT

A knight's most valuable piece of equipment was his warhorse—a highly trained animal known as a destrier. He also needed a packhorse and a riding horse called a palfrey for his travels. Before the 14th century, his main weapon was a sharp, doubled-edged sword. Until plate armor was invented (see page 6) long-sleeved chain mail shirts, called hauberks, and leggings were used for armor. A large shield displayed the knight's own coat of arms.

A knight's helmet, called a great helm or bucket helm, protected the head but had no air holes and was hard to see out of.

Knights would practice their cavalry charges at tournaments by jousting with lances. Tournaments were also a chance to show off their wealth and finery.

CRUSADING KNIGHTS

In 1095 Pope Urban II called for the Holy Land to be taken back from Muslims so Christian pilgrims could visit the site of Jesus Christ's tomb. Called "taking up the cross," many knights performed military service on crusades. In return, the Church forgave all their sins.

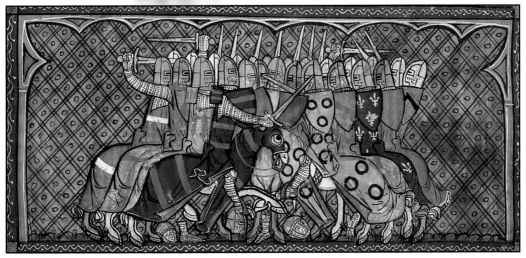

These 14th-century knights wear great helms and surcoats over their chain mail. They wield sharp, pointed swords that were very effective at piercing the rings of chain mail armor.

Knights in Battle

During the 14th century, pieces of plate armor, molded to fit the shoulders, chests and legs of knights, began to be used. Makers specializing in plate armor sprung up in Italy and Germany. By 1400 the rich, fashionable knight was dressed from head to toe in metal.

In 1346, English archers first defeated French knights at the Battle of Crecy in France.

A HUNDRED YEARS WAR

In 1328, with no clear heir to the throne of France decided, England's King Edward III declared himself king of France. In 1346, he invaded and won a great victory at Crecy. He also captured Calais, a strategic port for launching raids.

In 1356, his son, Edward, "the Black Prince," also invaded France and won another great victory at Poitiers. France fell into chaos. Edward III

This helmet from the 14th century is called a bascinet. A chain mail aventail, or collar, protected the throat. The best helmets also had snout-like visors.

invaded again, intending to be crowned at Reims. However, the town resisted his siege and all his gains, except for Calais, were lost.

Forty-five years later, the newly crowned King Henry V of England invaded while France was ravaged by civil war. After a struggle taking the port of Harfleur, Henry headed his troops toward Calais…

By 1429 England's conquest of France had reached as far as it would go. At the Siege of Orleans (left) a French peasant girl named Joan (below), led by visions from God, had an extraordinary effect.

WARS OF THE ROSES

Edward III created the first English dukedoms—territories given to the highest-ranking nobles—and awarded them to his sons making them hugely powerful. Edward III's eldest son, Edward, died a year before him, so his grandson became King Richard II. His overthrow would spark an epic feud between Edward III's descendants.

The two most powerful lines were the House of York (the white rose) and the House of Lancaster (the red rose). In 1399, Richard II was deposed, or overthrown as king, by his brother's son, Henry IV—a Lancaster. The Lancasters ruled until Henry VI was deposed by Edward IV—a York, who practically wiped out the Lancaster line at the Battle of Towton in 1461. The only challenger left was the heir Henry Tudor— a Lancaster.

The mace was a club-like weapon, effective at breaking through plate armor.

By the time of the battle at Bosworth (see page 32), the top knights were wearing full gothic-style plate armor. The helmet, called a sallet, had a long slit to see through. A metal chin-piece called a bevor protected the neck. The armor was made to be able to move at the joints. It was about as heavy as today's army gear.

The Battle of Agincourt

OCTOBER 25, 1415. THE OPEN LAND BETWEEN THE WOODS OF TRAMECOURT AND AGINCOURT IN NORTHERN FRANCE.

PREPARE TO ADVANCE.

AGAINST THE USUAL MILITARY STRATEGY OF THE TIME, ENGLISH KING HENRY V WAS MAKING THE FIRST MOVE AGAINST THE FRENCH ARMY SPREAD OUT BEFORE HIM.

AS THE ORDER TO ADVANCE PASSED THROUGH THE RANKS, EACH MAN FELL TO HIS KNEES, KISSED THE GROUND, AND PUT A SMALL PIECE OF EARTH IN HIS MOUTH.

MANY OF THE 9,000 MEN WERE SICK WITH DYSENTERY, AND ALL WERE TIRED AND HUNGRY.

AGAINST THEM STOOD AT LEAST 12,000 - THE CREAM OF THE FRENCH ARMY, BARRING THE ROUTE TO THE ENGLISH-HELD FORTRESS - AND REFUGE - AT CALAIS.

THE 7,000 ENGLISH LONGBOWMEN POSITIONED ON BOTH SIDES OF THE KNIGHTS HURRIEDLY PULLED THEIR PROTECTIVE STAKES OUT OF THE GROUND.

COME ON! COME ON! HURRY IT UP!

OOOF!

HENRY V GAVE THE ORDER.

LET'S GO!

AS 2,000 GLINTING MEN BEARING POLEARMS ADVANCED TOWARD THEM, THE KNIGHTS OF THE FRENCH VANGUARD BECAME ANXIOUS...

WHERE THE DEVIL ARE THE CAVALRY KNIGHTS?

SOMEWHERE IN THE REAR GIVING THE HORSES FORAGE. WE WEREN'T EXPECTING A MOVE LIKE THIS.

MEANWHILE THE BOWMEN RAN FORWARD AND REPOSITIONED THEIR STAKES IN FULL VIEW OF THE FRENCH SOLDIERS.

GRUNT!

HNNN!

BOK!

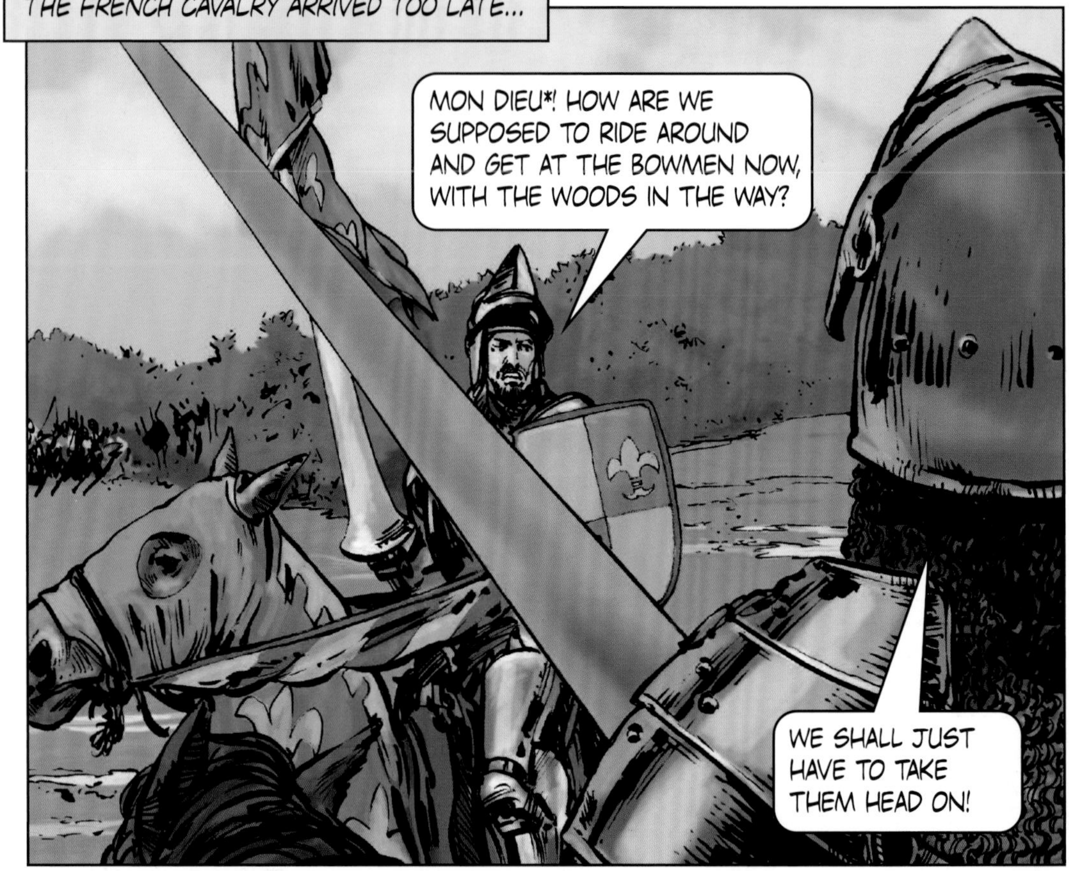
THE FRENCH CAVALRY ARRIVED TOO LATE...
MON DIEU*! HOW ARE WE SUPPOSED TO RIDE AROUND AND GET AT THE BOWMEN NOW, WITH THE WOODS IN THE WAY?
WE SHALL JUST HAVE TO TAKE THEM HEAD ON!

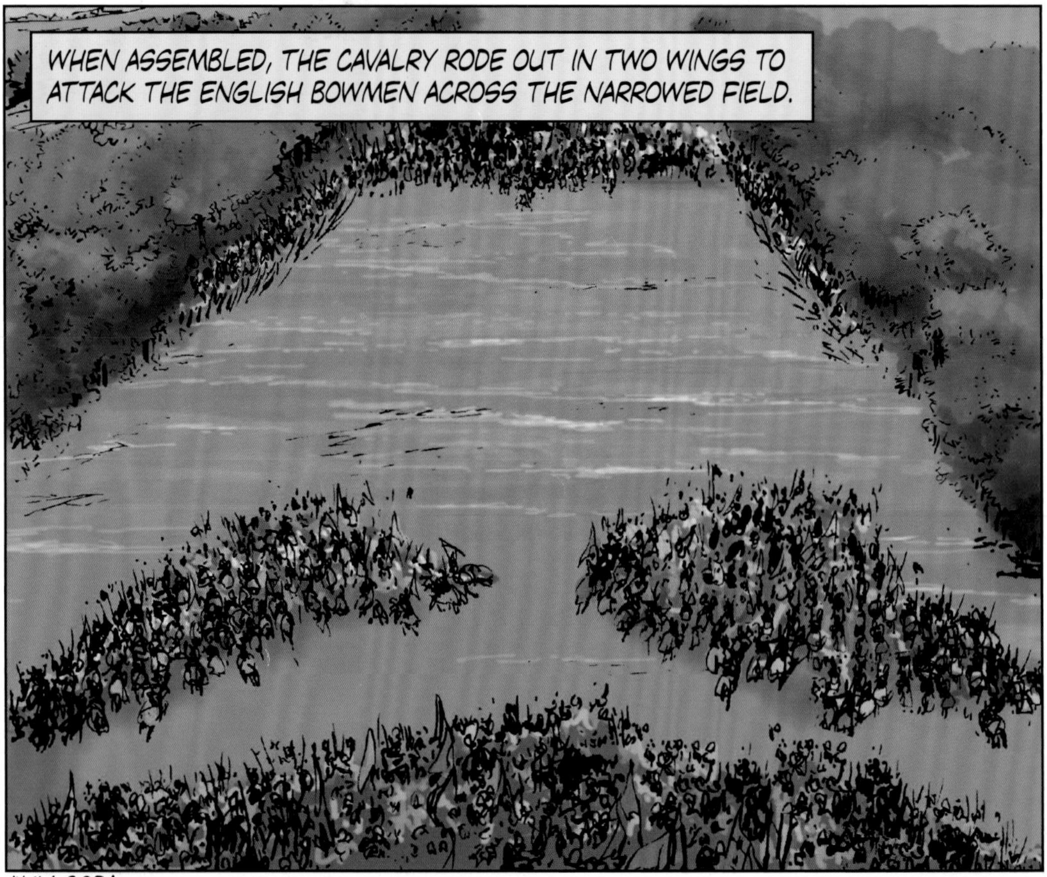
WHEN ASSEMBLED, THE CAVALRY RODE OUT IN TWO WINGS TO ATTACK THE ENGLISH BOWMEN ACROSS THE NARROWED FIELD.

*MY GOD!

THE FRENCH KNIGHTS' HORSES STRUGGLED THROUGH THE HEAVY CLAY.

IN THE VANGUARD THE MEN TRUDGED THROUGH THE RAIN-SOAKED GROUND, MADE WORSE BY THE CHURNING OF HUNDREDS OF HORSES' HOOVES.

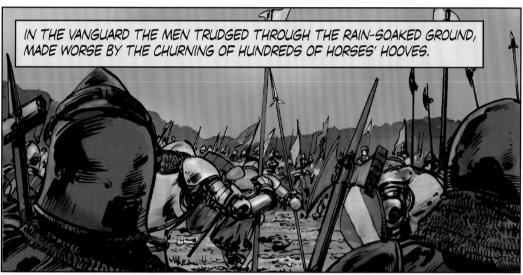

THE ENGLISH ARCHERS HELD THEIR BOWS READY, AND WAITED...

...FOR THE SIGNAL.

NOW, STRIKE!

ALL 7,000 RAISED THEIR BOWS AND FIRED.

IN AN INSTANT THE SKY WAS DARK WITH ARROWS...

AAAGH!

...FALLING LIKE DEADLY RAIN.

THE FRENCH CAVALRY SURVIVORS CRASHED UP AGAINST THE WOODEN SPIKES. HORSES WERE IMPALED; RIDERS FELL. THE CHARGE WAS COMPLETELY DRIVEN BACK.

WEEEHEEEEHEEEEE!

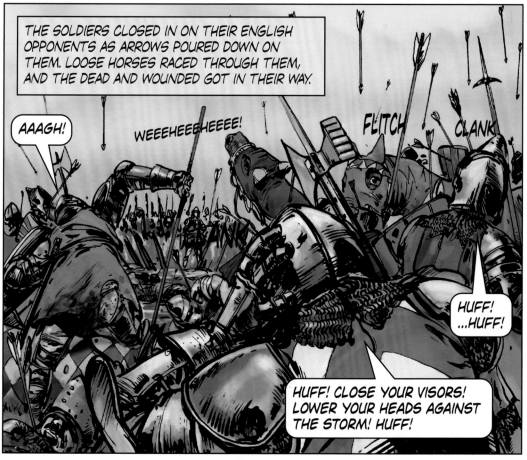

THE SOLDIERS CLOSED IN ON THEIR ENGLISH OPPONENTS AS ARROWS POURED DOWN ON THEM. LOOSE HORSES RACED THROUGH THEM, AND THE DEAD AND WOUNDED GOT IN THEIR WAY.

AAAGH!

WEEEHEEEHEEEE!

FLITCH

CLANK

HUFF! ...HUFF!

HUFF! CLOSE YOUR VISORS! LOWER YOUR HEADS AGAINST THE STORM! HUFF!

THE FRENCH FRONT LINE CRASHED INTO THE ENGLISH. MOMENTARILY THROWN BACK, THEY SURGED AGAIN. THE HAND-TO-HAND COMBAT WAS VICIOUS.

THE BOWMEN LEVELED THEIR AIM AND FIRED POINT-BLANK INTO THE CROWDS OF FRENCH KNIGHTS.

RAPIDLY THEY PICKED OFF TARGETS.

THUNK

FWUFFF...

AAAAAGH!

RAAAAAAAAAAAGH!

RAAAAAAAAAAAGH!

NO ARROWS LEFT, THEY DROPPED THEIR BOWS AND PITCHED IN WITH SWORDS, HATCHETS, AND MALLETS.

CLANGGG

THEY FOUGHT WITH BLIND FURY, KNOWING THAT NONE OF THEM WOULD BE SPARED AS PRISONERS IF THEY LOST THE BATTLE.

THE WORN OUT, SLOW-MOVING FRENCH KNIGHTS WERE AT THE MERCY OF THE ENGLISH SOLDIERS.

FIGHTING IN THE CENTER HENRY'S BROTHER, THE DUKE OF GLOUCESTER, SUDDENLY FELL FROM A VIOLENT THRUST.

ARRRGH!

WORD QUICKLY REACHED THE KING.

HUMPHREY!?

MEN! COME WITH ME!

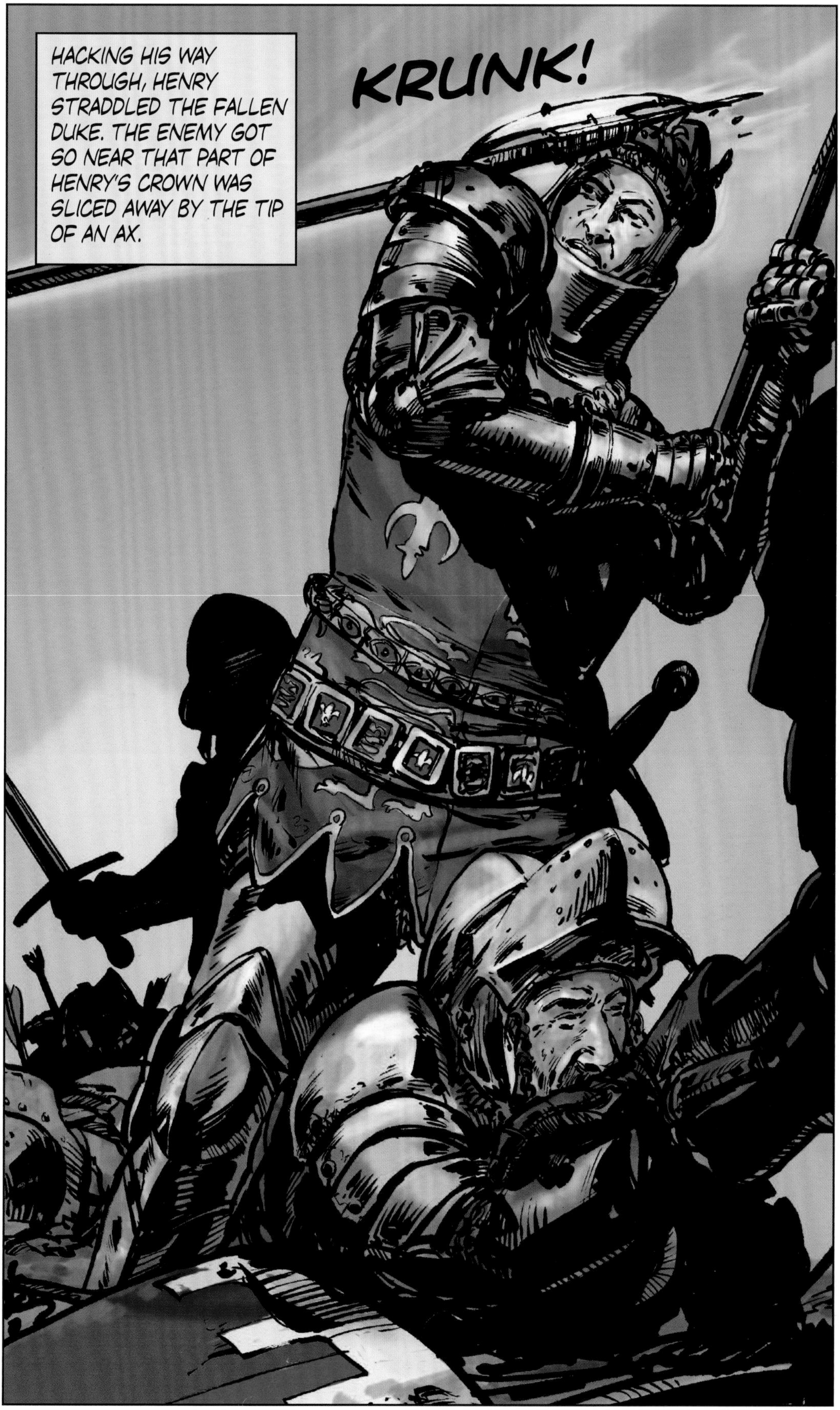
HACKING HIS WAY THROUGH, HENRY STRADDLED THE FALLEN DUKE. THE ENEMY GOT SO NEAR THAT PART OF HENRY'S CROWN WAS SLICED AWAY BY THE TIP OF AN AX.
KRUNK!

WAVE UPON WAVE OF FRENCH KNIGHTS SURGED FORWARD, HEEDLESS OF THE DEAD IN FRONT, EAGER TO GET AT HENRY AND AVENGE THE TAKING OF HARFLEUR.

KRIN...

WOOARGH!

NYAAAARGH!

SKUNCH

GUUURGLE...

THE PILE OF FALLEN IN FRONT OF THE KING'S STANDARD GREW ENORMOUS. AS THE LIVING FELL ALONGSIDE THE DEAD, MANY SUFFOCATED UNDER THE WEIGHT, OR WERE FORCED DOWN INTO THE MUD AND DROWNED.

AFTER THREE HOURS IT ENDED. ENGLAND HAD WON THE DAY AGAINST ALL ODDS.

ANYONE WITH A COAT OF ARMS, TAKE THEM PRISONER. THE REST, PUT TO DEATH!*

AN UNEXPECTED WIN! MAYBE I *WILL* BE KING OF FRANCE...

THE ENGLISH VICTORY WAS LEGENDARY – LESS THAN 200 ENGLISH LIVES LOST FOR THOUSANDS UPON THOUSANDS OF FRENCH.

*ANY PRISONERS WHO COULDN'T BE RANSOMED WERE THOUGHT TO BE WORTHLESS.

THE END

The Siege of Orleans

MAY 7, 1429. THE EFFORT BY THE FRENCH TO BREAK THE SIEGE OF ORLEANS IN NORTH CENTRAL FRANCE WAS NOT GOING WELL. THEY HAD BEEN INSPIRED BY FRENCH MAID, JOAN OF ARC, TO ATTACK THE ENGLISH-HELD FORT, THE TOURELLES, AT THE SOUTH END OF ORLEANS BRIDGE.

THAK!

AAAAAGHHH

THEIR ATTEMPTS TO UNDERMINE THE FOUNDATIONS OF THE WALL AND SET FIRE TO THE FORT'S BASTION HAD FAILED. IF ENGLISH REINFORCEMENTS ARRIVED, THE CITY WOULD FALL AND THE REST OF FRANCE COULD BE LOST.

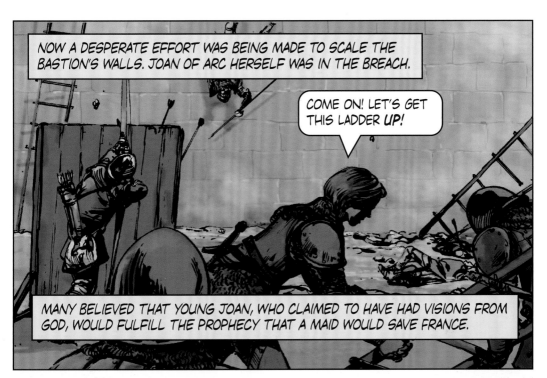

NOW A DESPERATE EFFORT WAS BEING MADE TO SCALE THE BASTION'S WALLS. JOAN OF ARC HERSELF WAS IN THE BREACH.

COME ON! LET'S GET THIS LADDER *UP!*

MANY BELIEVED THAT YOUNG JOAN, WHO CLAIMED TO HAVE HAD VISIONS FROM GOD, WOULD FULFILL THE PROPHECY THAT A MAID WOULD SAVE FRANCE.

DIRECTLY ABOVE, A CROSSBOWMAN TOOK AIM.

RIGHT! YOU WITCH...

...I HAVE YOU NOW!

23

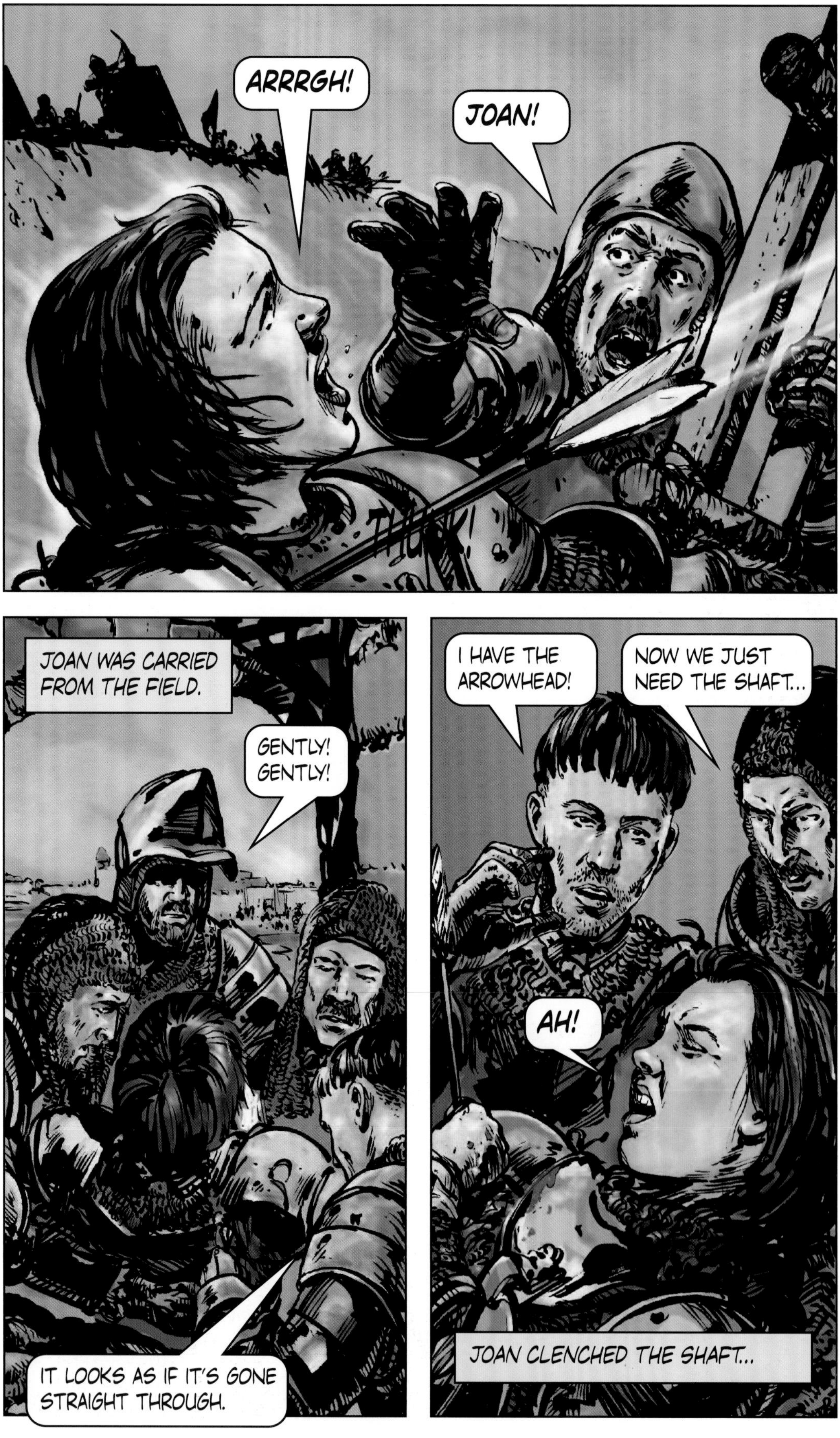
ARRRGH!
JOAN!
JOAN WAS CARRIED FROM THE FIELD.
GENTLY! GENTLY!
IT LOOKS AS IF IT'S GONE STRAIGHT THROUGH.
I HAVE THE ARROWHEAD!
NOW WE JUST NEED THE SHAFT...
AH!
JOAN CLENCHED THE SHAFT...

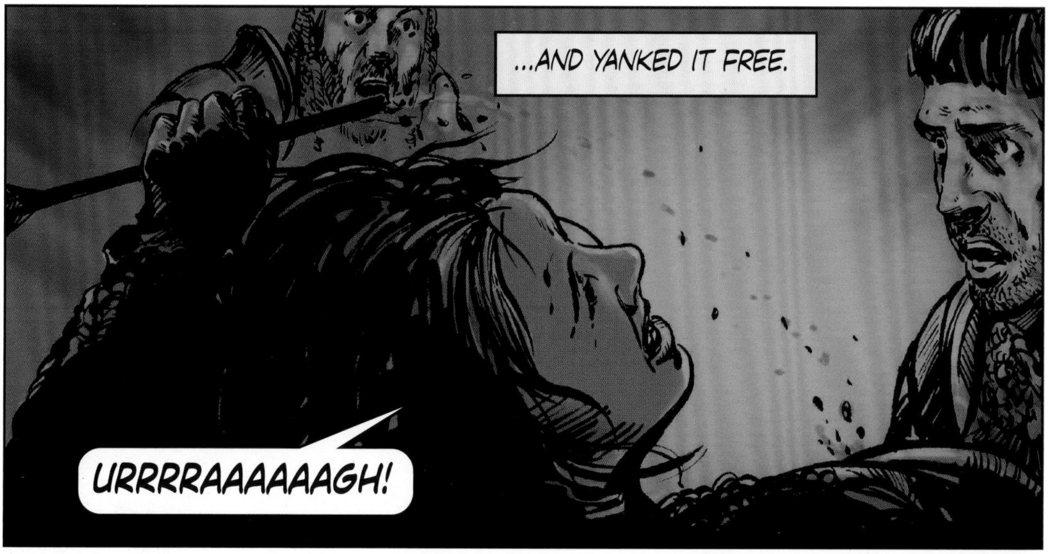
...AND YANKED IT FREE.
URRRRAAAAAAGH!

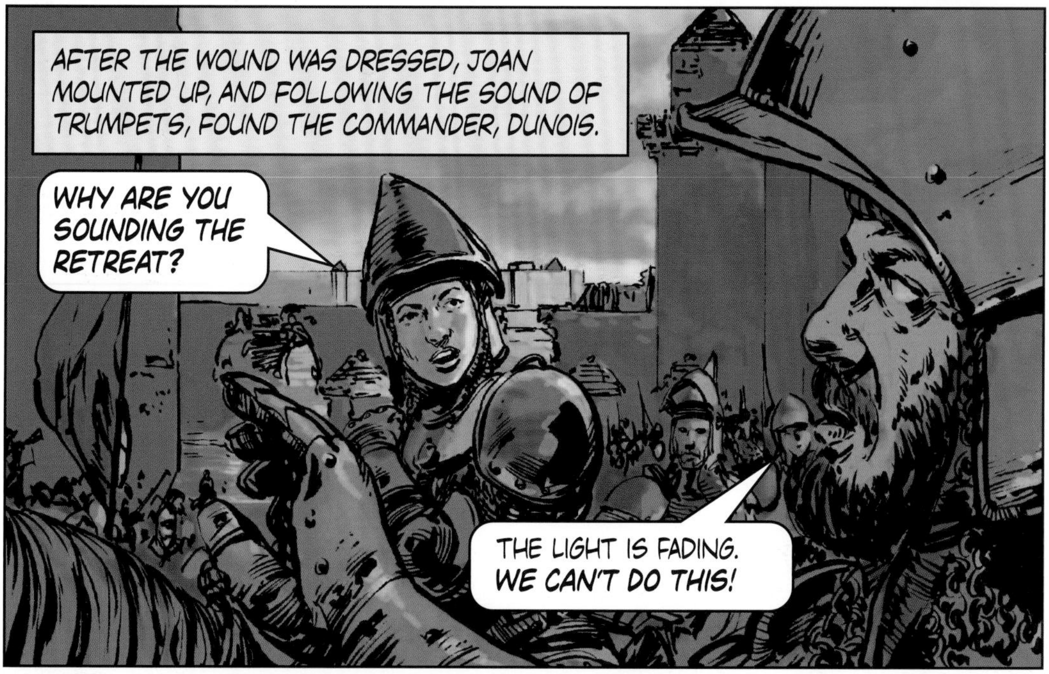
AFTER THE WOUND WAS DRESSED, JOAN MOUNTED UP, AND FOLLOWING THE SOUND OF TRUMPETS, FOUND THE COMMANDER, DUNOIS.
WHY ARE YOU SOUNDING THE RETREAT?
THE LIGHT IS FADING. WE CAN'T DO THIS!

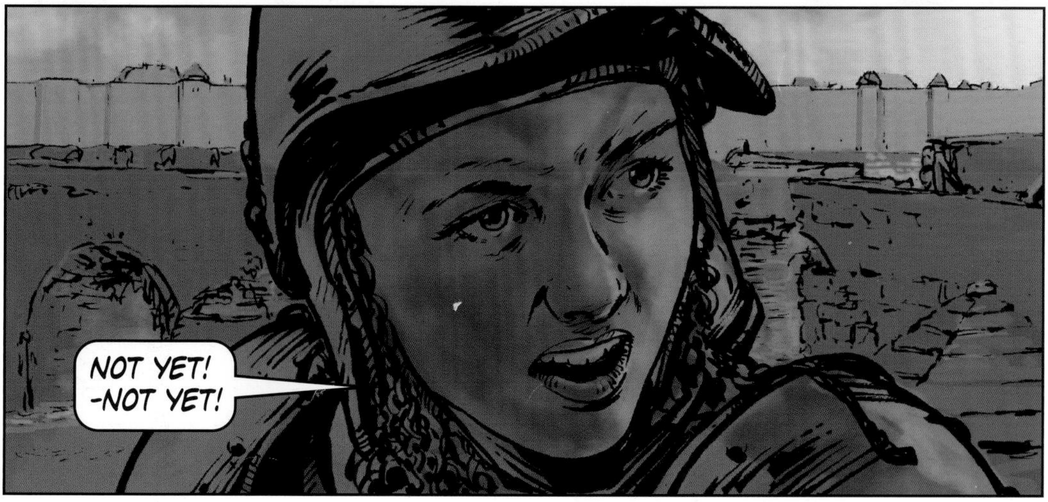
NOT YET! -NOT YET!

WHILE DUNOIS CALLED BACK THE MEN, JOAN WENT INTO A NEARBY VINEYARD FOR A QUIET MOMENT OF PRAYER.

COME ON! THE MAID SAYS WE HAVE TO RALLY.

SUDDENLY BURSTING FROM THE TREES JOAN SEIZED HER STANDARD AND GALLOPED TOWARD THE FORT.

DURRUM-DURRUM-DURRUM-

JAMMING THE STANDARD IN THE DITCH AT THE BASE OF THE WALL SHE SHOUTED WITH ALL HER MIGHT...

CHAAARGE!

AS THE MEN SWARMED UP THE LADDERS JOAN TURNED TO HER PAGE, DE CONTES.

RAAAAAA!

WHEN THE WIND CARRIES THE BANNER TO THE WALL, IT WILL BE OURS!

SWISSSHHH

NOW SMOKE WAS BILLOWING FROM THE RIVER SIDE OF THE BASTION.

EVERYONE, BACK TO THE KEEP!

THE WITCH - SHE'S ALIVE!

THE ENGLISH SOLDIERS RETREATED TOWARD THE TOWER - THEIR LAST REFUGE.

JOAN CAME FORWARD AND ADDRESSED THE BACK OF THE ENGLISH COMMANDER OF THE GARRISON...

GLASDALE, SURRENDER TO THE KING OF HEAVEN!

GLASDALE AND HIS KNIGHTS THUNDERED ACROSS THE BURNING DRAWBRIDGE TOWARD THE REFUGE OF THE KEEP ON THE RIVER.

OUT OF THE WAY!

THE BRIDGE SUDDENLY GAVE WAY, PLUNGING THE KNIGHTS INTO THE BARGE THAT BURNED BELOW.

AIEEEEEEEEEEEE!

MEANWHILE, ON THE OTHER SIDE OF THE TOURELLES, SOME OF THE FRENCH MILITIA LAID A ROUGH FOOTBRIDGE ACROSS THE BROKEN SPAN OF ORLEANS BRIDGE.

ALLEZ!* ALLEZ!

WITH THEIR CROSSING DISGUISED BY DARKNESS AND SMOKE, THE MILITIA SEEMED TO COME FROM NOWHERE TO SEIZE THE KEEP.

DROP IT!

*LET'S GO! LET'S GO!

THE NEXT DAY, THE ENGLISH CAME OUT OF THE FORTS SURROUNDING ORLEANS AND TOOK UP POSITIONS AS IF TO FIGHT, BUT THEN TURNED AND MARCHED AWAY.

WATCHING THEM LEAVE, JOAN WAS BOTH ELATED AND RELIEVED.

YES! THEY ARE RETREATING. LET THEM GO WHILE WE GIVE THANKS TO GOD!

THE RAPID AND UNEXPECTED VICTORY OVER THE BESIEGERS WAS THE SIGN JOAN HAD PROMISED THE DAUPHIN* AT POITIERS TWO MONTHS BEFORE. NOW HER MISSION WAS TO SEE HIM CROWNED KING OF FRANCE.

* FRENCH HEIR TO THE THRONE

THE END

The Battle of Bosworth

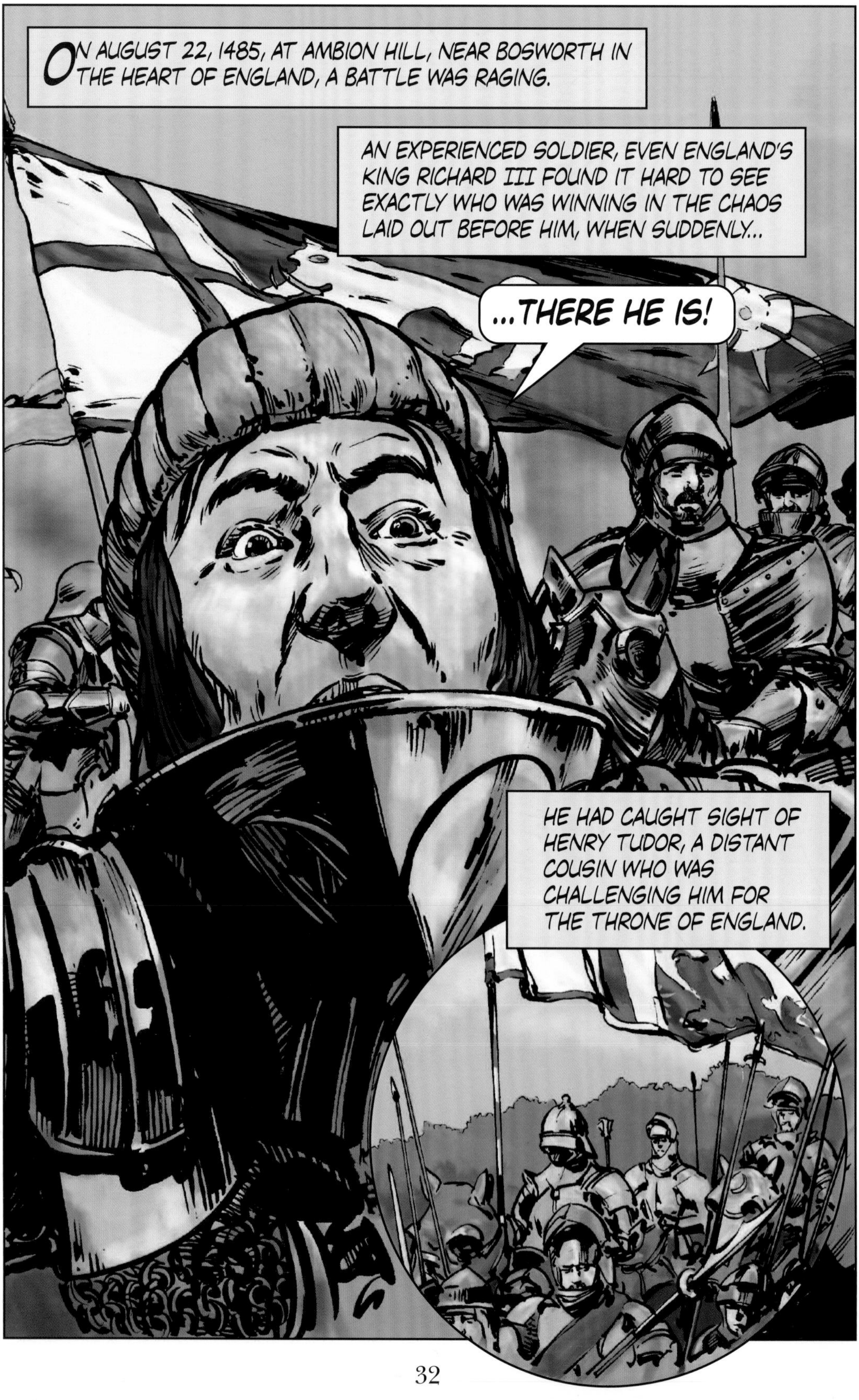
ON AUGUST 22, 1485, AT AMBION HILL, NEAR BOSWORTH IN THE HEART OF ENGLAND, A BATTLE WAS RAGING.
AN EXPERIENCED SOLDIER, EVEN ENGLAND'S KING RICHARD III FOUND IT HARD TO SEE EXACTLY WHO WAS WINNING IN THE CHAOS LAID OUT BEFORE HIM, WHEN SUDDENLY...
...THERE HE IS!
HE HAD CAUGHT SIGHT OF HENRY TUDOR, A DISTANT COUSIN WHO WAS CHALLENGING HIM FOR THE THRONE OF ENGLAND.

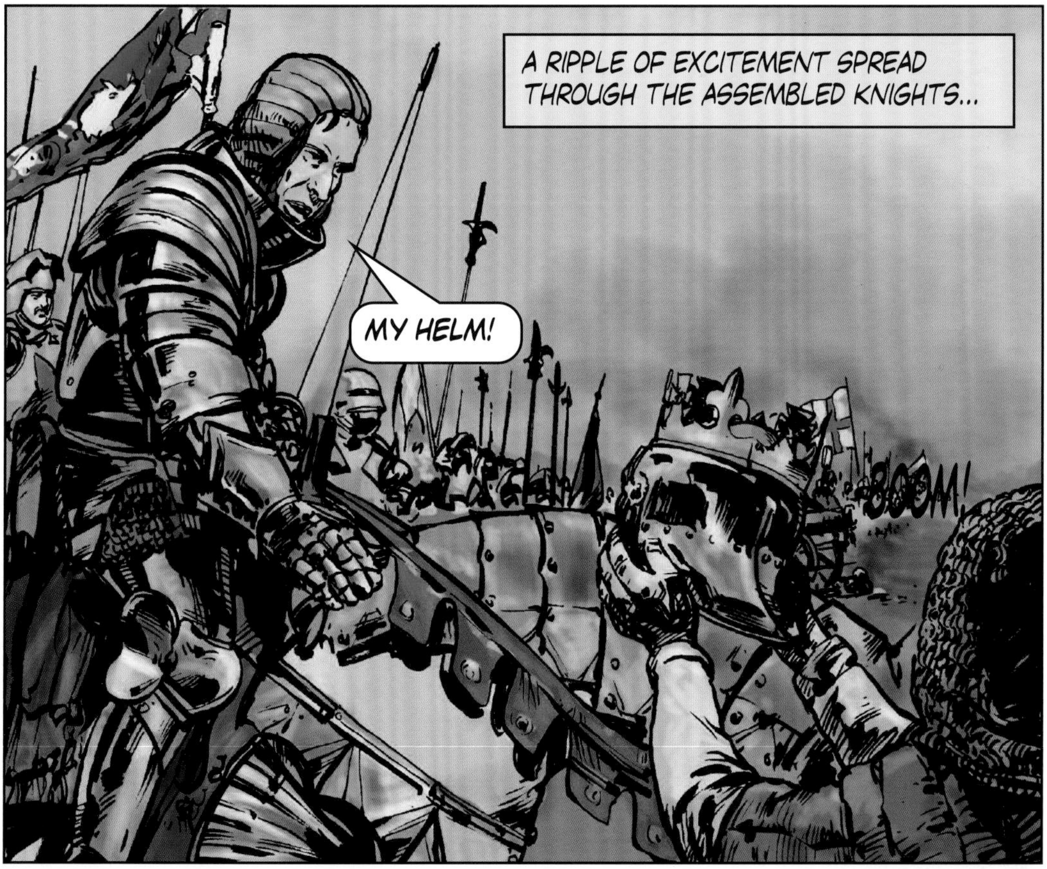
A RIPPLE OF EXCITEMENT SPREAD THROUGH THE ASSEMBLED KNIGHTS...
MY HELM!
BOOM!

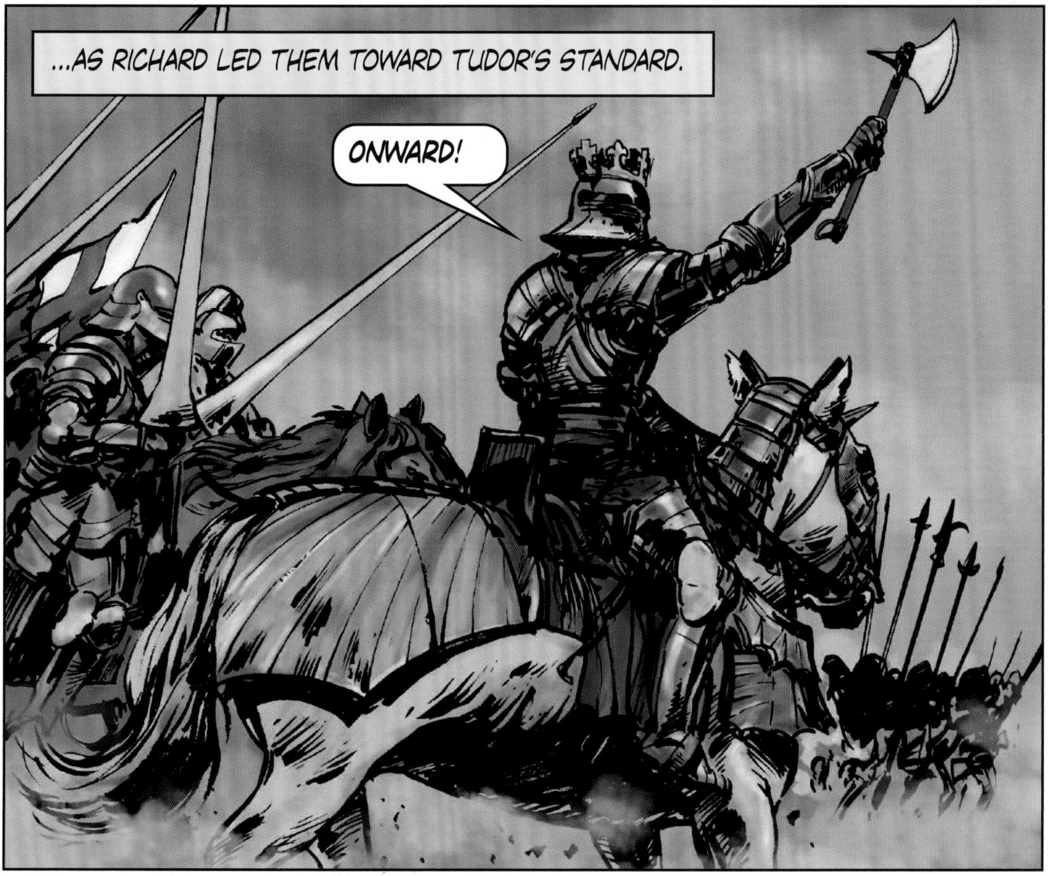
...AS RICHARD LED THEM TOWARD TUDOR'S STANDARD.
ONWARD!

CRUNCH

THE CHALLENGER'S SUPPORTERS ACTED QUICKLY.

TUDOR! GET DOWN OFF YOUR HORSE. WE WILL PROTECT YOU.

HENRY WAS NO WAR LEADER.

PIKEMEN AT THE REAR OF HIS FRONT TROOPS WERE ORDERED BACK AT ONCE...

FORM A SQUARE. PROTECT THE PRINCE!

...AND QUICKLY ARRANGED INTO A FORMATION BRISTLING WITH SPEARS.

UNLIKE RICHARD, TUDOR HAD BEEN FORCED TO HIRE A ROUGH BAND OF MERCENARIES, AND PIKEMEN "BORROWED" FROM FRANCE.

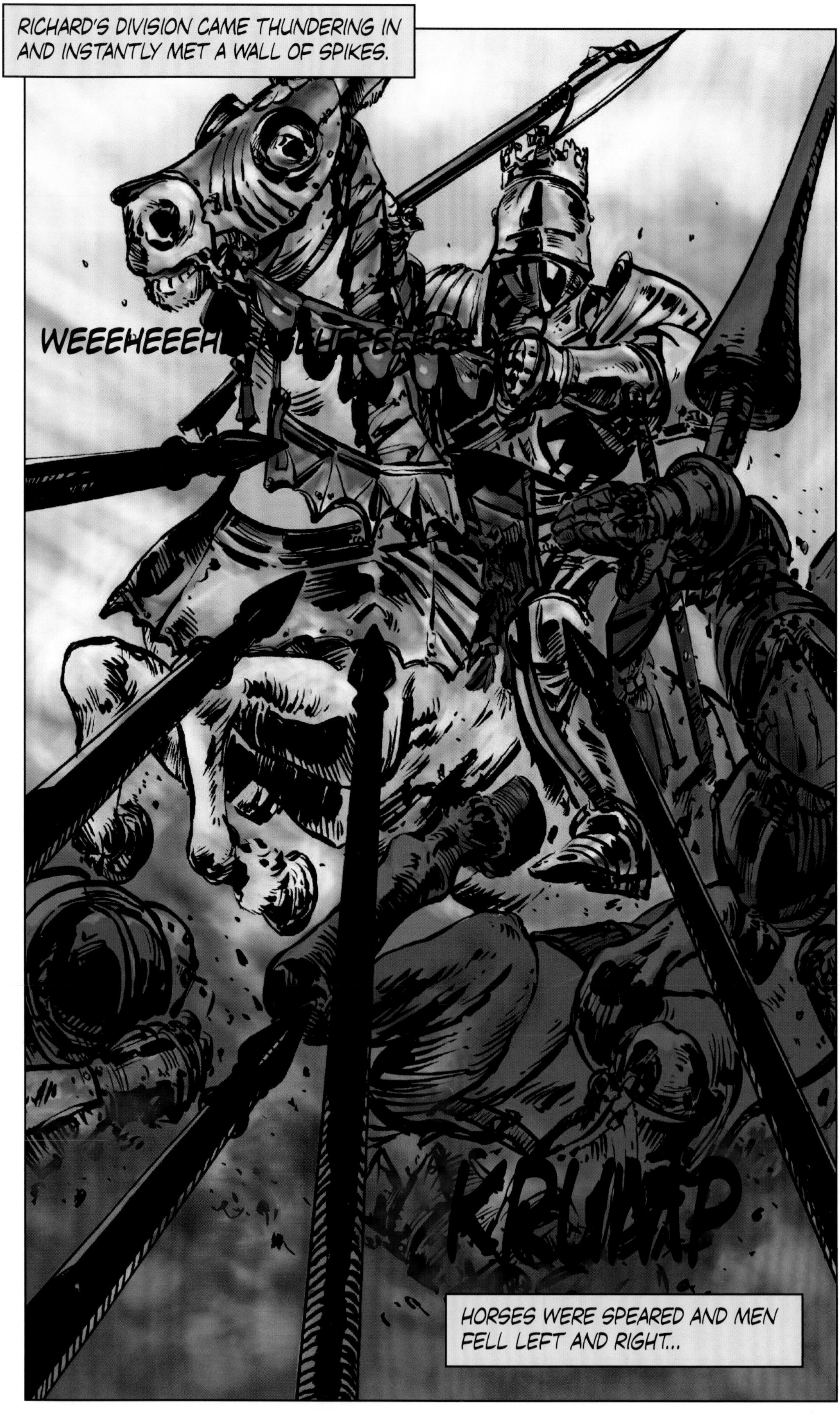
RICHARD'S DIVISION CAME THUNDERING IN AND INSTANTLY MET A WALL OF SPIKES.
WEEEHEEEEH
KRUMP
HORSES WERE SPEARED AND MEN FELL LEFT AND RIGHT...

...INCLUDING THE KING...

CURSE YOU!

THE FAILED CHARGE HAD BEEN WATCHED BY SIR WILLIAM STANLEY. HE HAD STOOD BY WITH HIS FORCE TO SEE WHETHER TUDOR'S MEN WOULD WIN.

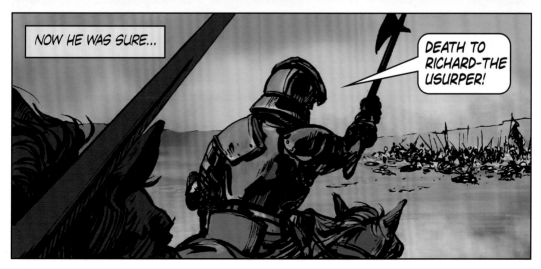

NOW HE WAS SURE...

DEATH TO RICHARD-THE USURPER!

FOLLOWING THE DEATH OF HIS BROTHER, KING EDWARD IV, RICHARD HAD BECOME ROYAL PROTECTOR TO EDWARD'S YOUNG SON, UNTIL HE BECAME OLD ENOUGH TO BE KING.

YOUNG PRINCE EDWARD AND HIS BROTHER, THE DUKE OF YORK, HAD BEEN TAKEN TO THE TOWER OF LONDON. GRADUALLY THEY WERE SEEN LESS AND LESS OFTEN, UNTIL THEY WERE SEEN NO MORE...

MEANWHILE, TO PREVENT EDWARD'S IN-LAWS FROM CLAIMING THE THRONE, RICHARD HAD MADE HIMSELF KING.

WHILE MANY PEOPLE WERE HAPPY FOR HIM TO BE KING, THERE WAS A SUSPICION THAT HE HAD MURDERED THE "PRINCES IN THE TOWER" TO TAKE THEIR THRONE. THE RUMOR LINGERED.

THE DOWNED KING WAS HELPED TO HIS FEET.

SIRE, WE'LL GET A HORSE AND TAKE YOU TO SAFETY!

A HORSE?

MY KINGDOM FOR A HORSE?

NO! WE WILL FINISH THIS!

KILLING TUDOR WOULD SECURE RICHARD'S RULE ONCE AND FOR ALL.

FIGHTING HAND TO HAND, RICHARD AND HIS REMAINING KNIGHTS BATTERED THEIR WAY THROUGH THE WALL OF PIKES.

KRUNK

ARRRRRRGH!

FINALLY, RICHARD REACHED TUDOR'S STANDARD BEARER...

NO! NO! BACK OFF!

...AND CHOPPED HIM DOWN.

THAK

WITH ALMOST SUPERHUMAN FURY, THE KING HACKED A PATH TOWARD HIS RIVAL...
HNNNGH!
WHUNK
NYAAAGH!
...HE WAS SO CLOSE...
...HE COULD ALMOST TOUCH HIM.
BUT NOW SIR STANLEY'S FORCES HAD REACHED THE BATTLE.

THE IMPACT OF STANLEY'S FRESH TROOPS WAS TOO MUCH. SUDDENLY, THE KING'S STANDARD BEARER WAS KNOCKED DOWN, SWIFTLY FOLLOWED BY THE KING HIMSELF.

WITHOUT HIS HELMET, RICHARD WAS HELPLESS TO RESIST THE FATAL, STABBING BLOW...

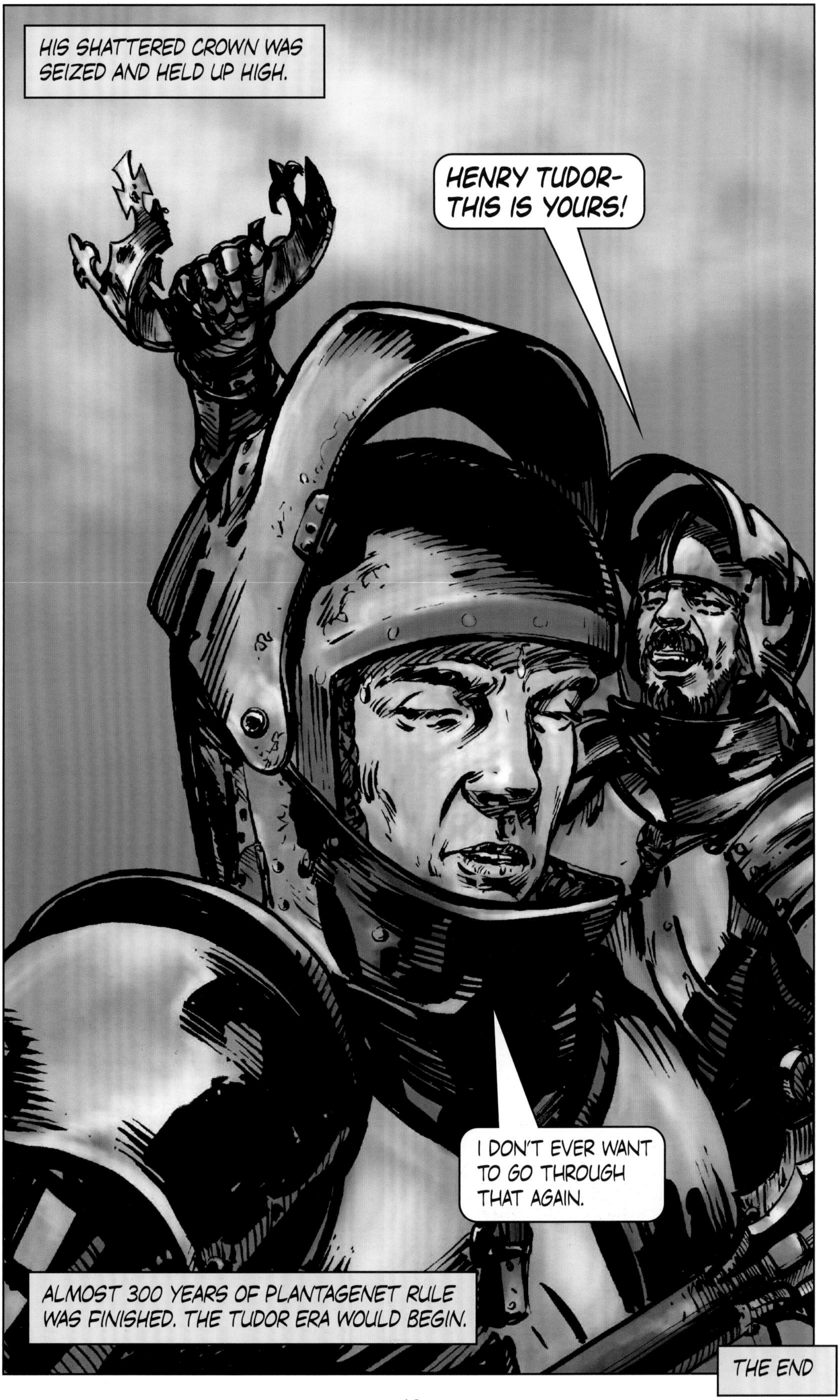
HIS SHATTERED CROWN WAS SEIZED AND HELD UP HIGH.
HENRY TUDOR- THIS IS YOURS!
I DON'T EVER WANT TO GO THROUGH THAT AGAIN.
ALMOST 300 YEARS OF PLANTAGENET RULE WAS FINISHED. THE TUDOR ERA WOULD BEGIN.
THE END

The End of Knights

A village elder's daughter, she became revered as the "knight" who inspired the last defense of France against English invaders. After the Battle of Orleans, Joan of Arc went to the dauphin and convinced him to travel to Reims to be crowned king of France.

DOWNFALL

Joan fought alongside French knights, conquering English forts that barred the route to Reims. At Patay, the English were waiting in ambush, with archers surrounding their defenses. But

A 19th-century painting shows Joan of Arc at the coronation of Charles VII.

French scouts reported their positions to the knights. The French attacked and caught the longbowmen by surprise, slaughtering thousands of English—their revenge for the loss at Agincourt.

King Charles VII (Charles the Victorious), was crowned king of France on July 17, 1429. Joan wanted to continue forcing the English from France, but on May 23, 1430, she was captured by Burgundians.

The Burgundians were allies of the English. They captured Joan and ransomed her to the English for 10,000 gold crowns. She was put on trial for heresy, found guilty, and burned at the stake in Rouen by the English, on May 30, 1431. Four hundred and eighty-nine years later, she was made a saint by the Church.

New Dynasty

Henry Tudor's claim to the English throne came through the line of his mother, who was a great-granddaughter of John of Gaunt. To strengthen his claim, Henry married Edward IV's daughter, Elizabeth of York. The marriage joined together the houses of Lancaster and York. He was crowned Henry VII on October 23, 1485, and reigned for 24 years.

Henry VII built up the navy and managed the administration, or running of the country, well. The new Tudor dynasty helped usher in the Renaissance era of advancement in arts, architecture, and learning.

Henry VII holds the Tudor rose—the roses of Lancaster and York combined. Well respected, he kept his nobles under control.

Honorary Knights

In the 15th century simple firearms were used for the first time. As these weapons developed, full plate armor became increasingly impractical and ineffective.

Knighthoods are still awarded by the monarch in the United Kingdom, but as honorary titles only. The highest honor is the Most Noble Order of the Garter, first awarded by Edward III.

Sometimes called the "last knight," Emperor Maximilian I of the Holy Roman Empire was famous for the detailed decoration of his armor.

Glossary

barge A broad flat-bottomed boat that is usually towed and used to transport goods in harbors and on rivers and canals

bastion A projecting part of a fortification, designed to give soldiers some protection while allowing them to fire

besiegers Surrounding armed forces for the purpose of capturing

breach A gap in the fortifications or line of defense of an enemy, created by the bombardment of attacking forces.

cavalry Soldiers who fight on horseback

chain mail Flexible armor consisting of small metal rings linked together

coat of arms The heraldic badge of a noble family, displayed on their shields and clothing in battle

chivalry The combination of qualities expected of an ideal knight, namely courage, honor, courtesy, justice, and a readiness to help the weak

Christian A person who believes in Jesus Christ and follows his teachings

dauphin The title given to the heir to the throne of France

deposed Overthrown and removed from a position of power

descendants A person, plant, or animal that is descended from a particular ancestor

dysentery A serious disease that causes diarrhea and loss of blood

elder A person of greater age and experience

elite A small powerful group of people

forage A search for food or supplies

Franks Members of a Germanic people living in ancient Gaul

freeman A rent-paying tenant who owed little or no service to the local lord

gallant Chivalrous, courteous, respectful, and polite

garrison The group of soldiers stationed in a fort or town in order to defend it

gothic Relating to an old style of architecture

heresy An opinion or belief that goes against the accepted religion of the time

Holy Land Palestine, an ancient country in southwestern Asia on the east coast of the Mediterranean Sea—a place of religious pilgrimage

Jesus Christ The source of the Christian religion and Savior in the Christian faith

keep The innermost and strongest part or central tower of a medieval castle

longbowmen Soldiers who used long, hand-drawn bows

medieval Relating to the Middle Ages

mercenaries Soldiers hired by a foreign country to fight in its army

Muslim A follower of Islam

noblemen A man of noble rank

page A youth in the Middle Ages being trained for knighthood and in the service of a knight

pikemen Soldiers armed with long thrusting spears known as pikes

pilgrims People who undertake a long journey to a sacred place or shrine

Plantagenet A royal dynasty that provided 14 kings of England during the Middle Ages

point-blank Aimed at a target from a very short distance away

polearm A long metal or wooden pole with an axe-like head used as a weapon in close combat

prophecy A prediction of what will happen in the future

red rose The House of Lancaster's badge during the Wars of the Roses

refuge A place that provides shelter or protection

Renaissance The revival of classical art, architecture, literature, and learning that originated in Italy in the 14th century and later spread throughout Europe, marking the transition from medieval to modern times

standard The banner or flag of a king or noble, carried into battle by a soldier called the standard bearer

undermine To dig out or wear away the earth beneath

usurper Someone who illegally takes the place of another; often taking the place on a throne

vanguard The front, or first, troops to engage in a battle

white rose The House of York's badge during the Wars of the Roses

Index